let the heart hold down the breakage

Or   the caregiver's log

let the heart hold down the breakage

Or   the caregiver's log

Maureen Owen

Hanging Loose Press,
Brooklyn, New York

Published by Hanging Loose Press, PO Box 150608, Brooklyn,
New York, 11215.

www.hangingloosepress.com

Printed in the United States of America 10 9 8 7 6 5 4 3 2 1

Acknowledgments
Some of these works first appeared in *Posit, The Brooklyn Rail, Blazing Stadium, Boog
City, Positive Magnets, Hurricane Review, The Café Review,* Joe Carey's art exhibition,
Hanging Loose, Exacting Clam, a Belladonna broadside, *Three Fold* and *Poets on the Road*
(pamphlet).

Special thanks to my granddaughter, Kayley, for two title inspirations. And a heartfelt,
grateful thanks to our family and friends and the loving neighbors and pals of my mother
in California, who were a deeply appreciated joy and support, who kept our spirits high,
who visited often, and who were always there for us.

Hanging Loose thanks the Literature Program of the New York State Council on the Arts
for a grant in support of the publication of this book.

Front and back cover drawings by Yvonne Jacquette
Book design by Nanako Inoue
Author photo by Rachael Pongetti

ISBN: 978-1-934909-72-0

This book is dedicated to my mom
DeLoris Catherine Phalen Tracy
"Protector of the Pines"
And to caregivers everywhere

In the U.S. 78% of adults in need of long-term care depend on family and friends as their only source of help.

During any given year, more than 65 million people, approximately 29% of the U.S. population, provide care for a chronically ill, disabled, or aged family member or friend.

Up to 70% of family caregivers manage medications for their loved ones.

Family caregivers suffer from stress, lack of exercise, depression, poor eating habits, deterioration of their own physical heath, and increased expenses.

She moves as paper moves
her skin upon the air

3

caregiver's log 4.2.18

Before it began my brother and I had chatted over the phone that I would come, visit him and family, then take my mom, who'd spent January, February, and March at his warm California, hilltop home, back up to her place in the high Sierras of Truckee. But some days later when he picked me up at the train station he announced with more than a little agitation that she wouldn't be able to continue living alone in her cabin. She had just gotten out of the hospital the day before and was not in good shape. I queried him about the cause of her hospitalization. We had celebrated her 95th birthday with a road trip to Monterey and Pacific Grove where two close friends of hers lived on California's coast. They were hosts paragraph excellence and we'd had a fabulous time visiting them and celebrating Mom. That was the week of February 21st. I had just retired from my job on February 2nd and went home to continue setting up my new life with the plan that I would come in April after the snow let up in Truckee to help mom get home and set up her house. Then my mom had some breathing issues in mid March and my brother had to take her for a short hospital stay. She been out of the hospital and feeling better when, right before my arrival, she'd developed a cough and had to go back into the hospital for a couple of nights. Now he had just brought her home the day before my arrival. I wasn't sure how to respond to his announcement that she couldn't continue living alone. Well, Let me see how she is, I offered. I felt blindsided by sternly delivered, his open ended news.

When we arrived we went directly down to see mom.

My brother, some years earlier, had built a lovely one-room living space for my mom's winter visits down some moss-grown, rustic steps on the lee side of the hill, just past the garage. The main house sets on the hilltop and beams a California Shangri-la status of lush cactus and rosemary, lemon and lime trees, and a wide front room window that looks out over a greenery of eucalyptus, lawns and wild bushes, horse pastures, a little town, a gambling casino, small farms, and further into a distant low range of mountain beyond which lies the sea. The cabin sports a sweet wrap around porch and nestles under one of the huge oaks that protectively hover over the buildings. I do believe my brother built it for our mother, but it was christened the Hunter's Shack immediately and hung with several deer head trophies from my brother's hunting trips and that my sister-in-law was delighted to get out of the house. The deer heads were many and stuffed quail and wild geese soon joined the defunct menagerie. Because the cabin sat vacant for most of the year, it gradually became a storage space for surplus household items.

My mom was seated on the couch at the far end of the room. The shutters were open and a staggered light filtered a green glow through the oak leaves. A little kitchenette with a microwave and small fridge tucked beside a bar wondrously constructed of big glass bricks greeted to the left and to the right a pop-out glass display bay window followed by a huge bed then an armoire and a wood burning stove enclave of round grey river rocks with an electric heater. In the middle of the room an oval table surrounded by 4 matching, bulky, wooden-carved chairs claimed center stage. I hugged my mom who was terribly thin, pallid as a sheet, and looked like she hadn't moved since my brother brought her home from the hospital the afternoon before.

It was April 2nd. I moved into the Hunter's Shack to take care of her.

She was never "herself" from that day
I came into the hunter's shack & marked
her across the room

"I'm so glad you're here,"
she managed

**Smacked once   severely on the nose   left me
rolling   to the far outside   of the bed**

It was the much-needed rainy season and the rains began.

That first night it was already sprinkling when Mom and I left the main house
after dinner and a Hallmark episode of "Murder She Wrote." I walked in front
holding her hand, a bright flashlight in the other and my brother behind us shined
his flashlight as we crossed the driveway, skirted the garage and descended down
the moss soft stairs, pocked now with wet slippery oak leaves. My brother left us
inside the door and, ducking the thickening rain, trotted back the way we'd come.

Turning the electric heater up to high, I got Mom dried off and into her flannel
LL Bean pjs and fleece-lined slippers. Helped her wash up and brush her
teeth and then climb into bed. Climb is the appropriate word. The bed was a
white elephant in the room, literally. Huge, covered with a snowy white down
comforter, it seemed the parts of more than one bed had been requisitioned to
create its mismatched bulk. The headboard leaned not quite snugly against the
wall, the mattress came up against it at an unfortunate angle hanging slightly
over the bedsprings on all sides. A bountiful, solid mattress that could have been
enough by itself, now combined with the bedspring and frame, rose to a lofty
aerie. But it had been a long, exhausting day and once I loosed into its warmth
my critique of its artlessness vaporized and I felt as though sinking into the
puffiness of a vast marshmallow.

But that night and the nights that followed had other than rest in mind.

Her eyesight failing, my mother needed several of the dimmable ceiling lights
left on quite brightly. Also the lamp on her bed stand. And the bathroom light.
A rich golden glow one sees in the paintings of 17th century Dutch masters
infused a specific focus into the room, polishing the wooden table, reflecting
in the glass bar. Two of the ceiling fixtures beamed blindingly into my eyes. I
pulled a tangle of covers over my head.

Tho we'd raised her pillows, mom's breathing was labored and interrupted by outbursts of violent coughing fits. Suddenly from a restless sleep she would ratchet straight up forward from the bed, flailing her thin arms in all directions, hacking so piteously it seemed the air in the room ripped into strips. A tiny skeleton whirling, jerking, her skin transparent in the eerie amber light. Trying to help, I brought cough drops, held water to drink, handed her Kleenex. At last she would lie back, slowly drifting into a kind of dream she whispered and spoke from brokenly. After each bout I would ease into my side of the bed, attempting not to disturb her, lie without moving, and stare up into the wooden beams.

Through all it had begun to rain in earnest, a pouring rain, thrashing across the skylights, wailing against the cabin shutters. A trio of embalmed geese hanging on fishing line near the skylight, wind & thunder outside stirring their dusty feathers, bounced a little veering in flight. Were the taxidermied quail shuddering? It was impossible not to hear a scratchy hum of tiny shuffling claws panicking. Mounted deer head eyes moistened and I couldn't help but feel they were staring at us. Cobwebs in their antlers gusted ever so slightly; their soft noses so black, so still.

Night after night it rained.
Was I in hell?
Night after night for a solid month.
Then I took her home with me.

Mom

She wears my flip flops
In mid afternoon sun
I shade her ankles & feet
with my shadow

the pines nap too
still & drowsy   in their altitude
as a baby breathes   soft &
scarcely
it hurts my neck but I can't stop
staring up at them   their
glassy needle tops bristle   rolling   heaving
sea above

Dazzle Camouflage

Green that goes straight up   tousled locks of branches
then green as still as baize   firs and pines
the great green cargo of these branches   in layers   thick
green hunks of rafts   of forest   pitch and foam

kids across the way put up a makeshift stand
by the side   of the road   shake dust from
little trucks & chant   "Toys
for Sale!"   they plan to buy ice cream with the money

placing cloth chairs in the sun for her   moving to dappled
shade   when sun too hot   then back to sun when shade too cool
try to find a level spot for her chair in slantedness
move small table for water with chair   keep moving as sun
moves   tall shadows of the pines

screeching Steller jays   Dark-eyed Junco

no summer insects sing not one   utter silence breaches

it's the bottom of the 8th Giants up &   leading 3 to 1

"the queen is a triangle
the knight is a right angle
the bishop diagonal

moving   the pawn is like the queen
only lesser"   she said

the pines look wooly   up November's air
She rolls her hand in crisp leaves
under her chair
What are you looking for?
My glove
You have both your gloves on
Oh   I thought   I dropped one

they called from Mongolia   as they were   digging up the bones

It's about poverty
and how the poor   are used   to sell things to the rich
(as models for fashion   as vivid colorful shabby chic)   as

peppered & parsleyed with timber   behind us the snowed hills stratify
an occasional slab of river emerging glitter   from the ice

herds of cattle   knee-deep
in snow   gather   at an alfalfa hay drop

a painting made this   doubt
a swarm of chunks   of cirrus   nods
to curlicues

getting mad at anger   is counterproductive

it's really about tricksy   like her

squirrels swoop the green bunches   the pines
sway hypnotically   their branches hover and bounce
deep layers float and bob   swirl in murmuration

we get mail today   at last!
a jar of face cream
our skin is saved!

"Did you call Nancy?"

"We'll call her a little later," I say

"Are we late?"   my mother asks

Distortions   *for lg & cs*

vast white ruffles of cloud
bustling   dense   whipped
froth

rich fuzz of tawny   & slipping green
banks as tho herds of seals
sprawled   soft & sloping   hills

dyeing her long black hair   black

I dyed my mother's hair. I was 9 or 10 and we were too poor for her to frequent
a salon. My mother had beautiful long black Irish hair, but she had gone white
suddenly in her late 20's. I would pin my own frizzy, reddish hair back from my
face, don big Playtex yellow gloves, and put on an apron. My mother would mix
the magical Lady Clairol formula that smelled of hydrogen peroxide, put the
same black-spattered blue towel over her shoulders, and hand me the bulbous
squeeze bottle and her comb. We'd set up in the bathroom, rigging up a bright
commercial, aluminum-capped hanging bulb. I had a special washcloth to wipe
off quickly any black splotches I squirted on her forehead or ear tips or on my
own arms. I would part a section of her hair, lay a careful line of the black dye
to the roots of the part then comb it in and up and down the long strands. After,
we'd let it set in for an instructed length of time. Then, with me still wearing the
oversized gloves and she still in her blue towel, we'd go to the larger kitchen sink
and I would kneel on a chair and give her a sudsy shampoo and rinse out all the
extra dye. Bending over her shoulders and neck I could see the black strands flow
apart and the white of her scalp emerge in tiny winding rivers.

Scarf Washing Day
nightly

At bedtime I mix in a Japanese sake cup a few drops of lavender with a small amount of olive oil and massage it into the bottoms of her feet, up and around each toe, and over the instep arch, paying special attention to the heel's rough sides.

On her frail shoulders and curved back I gently rub Sarna lotion and down over her bow bent ribcage and into the soft tissue at the nape of her neck. Sarna with its soothing creaminess and ability to lightly numb the skin against itchiness in the night.

I would become the black sheep
of the family

obliquely   included

When I sneeze   she jolts &
flutters   "Why are you sneezing! What makes you sneeze?"
"Everyone sneezes once in a while," I say
"You sneeze all day." My mother charges
"No I don't. I rarely sneeze"
"Oh," she snaps, "you sneeze all the time!"

a recurrence whenever I do sneeze   or cough   so that
I've become self conscious about sneezing or clearing my throat.
I contort to prevent my sneezes   I begin to count them
Am I sneezing too often?   This has
never occurred to me before.

"My stomach is on fire!   I heard on tv
that if you rub your stomach from side to side   it will cool down."
She would sit   rubbing her stomach   east & west

Or

days of collywobbles

Good Morning!
Shower day!
        warm housecoat   slippers
        cane
        slowly we count 10 steps downstairs to walk-in shower
        carrying 1 special shampoo   3 towels
I set water temperature   just so
she stands showering   an ancient warrior   in a wild gale
we fold the glass door open
so I can assist   sponge back   suds hair
hand her a white face washcloth   then her brown body washcloth
a dry cloth for rivulets in her eyes
waters dripping from my sleeves and clothes
hop step her to a towel draped chair   I wrap and dry as quick
as possible   to ward off shivering   she so particular that I towel between each toe
then back up counting stairs   for lotions crèmes and clothes
on sunny days   we sit on porch settee   or
backyard chair w/pillows   to dry
and comb her fine white hair   as sailing breezes brush it
flouncing   like sun   on arctic snow

the Irish tray

   atop the ottoman   next her chair

Daily   on a map of our travels   her oximeter,
gum, measured water cup w/ice,   emery board, box of
Kleenex, 2 exercise squeeze balls, a magnifier,   8 ounce
can of spicy diced tomatoes for weight lifting,   talking time
clock,   tube of rose acacia hand cream,   Japanese fan,
box of toothpicks,   container of Tums,   an exercise
stretch band,   & a   blue ink   pen

she could put on her left ear hearing aid
but not   her right   & sometimes
          she could not put on her left either

back then
she would swing me up behind the saddle of the smokey mustang
go full gallop up the cow pasture till the very end fencing
my skinny arms wound around her waist for dear life   bounced
and flung   my sides pinching & aching
then   turn and gallop back through the cows   leap up the ditch   trotting
the gravel driveway   back into the yard

I become her human pack mule

preparation for a walk around the lake   the park   the block

her tan safari jacket
Kleenex in the pockets
sunscreen applied
Rio 2016 Olympics visor cap
or brimmed lavender hat
warm gloves
ice in water bottle
light long-sleeved shirt
sunglasses
cough drops
purse
gum
toothpick
her cane

if you can   paint sound
        you can write paint

I cook us dinner. Mom helps set the table.
Her food has to be piping hot.
I heat her plate in the microwave   spoon veggies
steaming from a pan on the stove   chicken dish straight
from the oven   we come to our meal   but after a few bites
"Is this supposed to be cold?" she raises.
"No,   I'll warm it up in the microwave,"   taking
her plate into the kitchen.
Not able to see well   on many a bite   her empty fork
goes into her mouth   she chews it anyway   refusing help
eating becomes a long   slow process   again
and again   "food's too cold."   I reheat and reheat her dinner

fresh water with ice   served dessert   dinner finished
found SF 49ers football game on tv for her
I'm back in kitchen   cleaning up   doing dishes
She's hollering now   "It's too loud!   I'm too
close to the tv. Too loud! Are you listening to it in
the kitchen?"
"No, I can't hear it in the kitchen."
I adjust the tv sound   "I think it was just the commercial,
so much louder than the game," I say
resuming dishes   but pitched now into the sudsy flow
swirling   out of control down the dark cavern of the drain's
wash   its rushing fall   hurling through forests of pipes   in
the black earth   below us

Cutting celery on a curved surface

Sometimes   out walking
we go   so slow
I almost   fall over

perfection isn't stable

as though ascending in an elevator
enormous white of Kleenex   floating   cubes
rectangles of it   kitchen counters   bedside table   trays
bureaus dresser tops   her
pockets airy stuffed   of blouse and pants jackets pjs   coats & vests

piled   four pillows high
steep hill of feathers
mauve sighs between
a thin red satin ribbon sewn
nightly   toppling

folding her boxy blue&white striped
embroidered   w/ tiny cobalt palm trees   swaying
long after she wore his black t-shirts to bed
her seersucker pants   faded cowboy shirt snap buttons
ribbing on the cuffs   kept

yellow doorway trapezoid
"Who is that boy," she queried
puffs of smoking pigment   rising   spread
a geography   of colored liquid
through his burning clothes

when baptismal waters   flow a
neon river   round our feet

I get up in early darkness   in
still night a.m.
retrieve my computer   &
hop back into bed with my mom
together we watch NASA's lander *InSight*
launch off to Mars

(She born 1923 on a Minnesota prairie farm
without electricity or plumbing
Now, her grandson on the NASA team)

I said "sandwich wraps"
   She thought I said "salmon traps"

How about soup for dinner?
What kind of soup?
Chicken Pot Pie soup.
O yes!
heat soup / set table
set up oxygen
What are you doing?   she asks between breaths
Making soup.
What kind of soup?
Chicken Pot Pie soup.
O Good!
Are there crackers?
Sure thing.
It's ready to eat.
What are we having?
Soup.
What kind of soup?
Chicken Pot Pie soup.
Take your time it's hot.
This is good. What is it?
Chicken Pot Pie soup.

With company she's engaged   no need
of oxygen   delighted   in conversation
She navigates the stairs &   eats without complaint

"Air   I need air!" pulling on her blouse
I switch on the ceiling fan   open the
front door   push up 2 windows wide   dial
swamp cooler blower to full blast
"I can't feel any air!" she's loud with gathering
agitation   I roll the swamp cooler closer to her
Kleenexes twirl upward from their box   magazines
rustle & blow open   the curtains ripple
"Do you feel air now?"
"Yes, yes, I can feel a little now   it's only blowing
on my arms though   on my legs   I need it up here"
she gestures to her face

I hammer down a nail in the floor that over time
has crept up
"What are you doing pounding?"
"A little nail head was sticking up."
"How do you know it was sticking up?"
"I could see it."
"Oh,   and you couldn't see it before?"

even when without lodgings

Dark racetrack quiet   everyone absorbed   thoroughbreds nodding   we'd
drive   back to the barns   find a vacant stall   a kindly loaned tack room
or empty horse van   to sleep in   gathering towels and toothbrushes
and from a spigot at the end of the shed row   she'd monitor our ablutions
our scrupulous brushing of teeth

I sleep on the pull out couch bed to be closer to her at night
Wickedly uncomfortable   lumpy   iron bar structure underneath
the attached tag says   "Cloud Mattress"

Nights were the worst.
Tired, she'd begin her panic
"I don't have enough air. There's not enough air in here.
Are the windows open? The door?   Is the fan on?"
yes to all I'd assure her   but she'd gasp
"I can't breathe!   Can't get enough air!
I need the nose thing!"   her request
for the oxygen tube   often she'd not use words
just wild eyed & arms flinging   gesticulating gasps
once hooked up to the generator   she'd question
"Is it working?   Is it on?   I don't feel any air.   I
don't hear it!"

I'd check the settings twice   assuring her
"It's ok   just   breathe"

billionaires   don't care if we like them

**   or**

that body that
her mouth made   a sound like a siren
way off   in the distance

times between her needing me   abbreviate
I could just go into the kitchen   soap a sponge
begin to scour around a burner   3 to 4 minutes
& her voice   would be calling me
I'd go see what she needed   return & wash the
second burner   her call
when back I'd scrub the 3rd
some nights I'd take items out of utility & silverware drawers
lave out & lay clean wax paper   then replace each spatula
corkscrew   cooking fork   ladle   slotted spoon   can opener
beer pick   back   in exquisite index   or
select a particular fridge shelf   set everything off   discard
old leftovers   rinse the shelf   & organize replaced items   in status
of height   I'd plan for the brief vain intervals
moving quickly   working   in stages

that sound of her falling cane

Her cane falls   off   table lips
off tops of chairs   from sofa arms
off breakfast hanging places   slides
a leaning arc along walls   walking
slaps the sidewalk   a singular crack
of contact

**I imagined she was not my grandmother's daughter
but conceived bone immaculate out of the Minnesota prairie
born on horseback**

3:50 a.m.   Bergman's hour of the wolf
hall light in my eyes   a squeaky rasp
"My back is killing me   it's so itchy
can you rub my back   put some cream on   rub
my shoulders   the bottoms of my feet
my arms   rub my thumb   my thumb is so itchy
Do I have a pulse?"
her small frail skeleton wisps   syllables in bits
crystallize cold dawn
                    "I'm sorry I had to wake you."

                    "It's alright."

**The oxygen generator buffs   plunges   a sea exhausted
falling ashore**

"Where did this water come from?" she suspicions
at dinner   referring disdainfully to her water glass

"It's our tap" I say   "we have really fine tap water.
Do you need another ice cube?"

"I can't drink it   it tastes bad."

"It's the same water we drink all the time"   I offer

"Tastes bad!   what else do we have?   is there
any juice?"

"yes   I got you the cranberry blueberry juice"

"I'll have that."

there's a second way to measure the distance to galaxies

She's coughing   retching
deferring   waste basket
easing into bed   stacking
pillow pyramid defying
gravity   arranging fans
window airs   staging
night lite   clipped on lantern
bulbs aglow   holding
hands   bed stand rosary
all subsiding   she into
ceasing   lifts her eyes
asks   "Do we have bacon?"

This morning woke

to mom calling me. Her pillows had collapsed again. I restacked them and helped
her back into bed, arranging the oxygen noseband and pulling up Sandy's floral
handkerchief quilt over her feet. Her face became so unlined and peaceful. The
grimace that had gathered of late faded. Her feather-white hair puffed around
what suddenly was a calm & peaceful brow. She looked angelic & beautiful. So
unusual as she mumbled, "air   Need more air   I can't breathe," but in a saintly,
even though desperate, quietness. "Is the oxygen on?" She pushed off the sheet
and blanket, "too much on me." I held her hand urging gently and breathed
with her to calm the panic that often caused her breathing problems and then the
gasping that would cause more panic. I sat as she drifted into a tender sleep. I
thought for a moment that her sudden serenity meant she might be dying.   Then I
tucked her in   and went barefoot   out into the grass   while she slept on.

**I thought you'd be just who you were   when
  I saw you last**

She wakes up in distress
eyes closed   is she awake?
gasping   murmuring inarticulately
"Do you want water?"
her mouth wide open looking so dry
she shakes her head   no water   she seems
to say   I prop her into sitting position
throw more pillows behind her
"water   my mouth so sore," she appears
to say   but then again refuses the straw
I rub her back
she is in acute distress   mumbling loudly
then   "water   water,"   again
this time she takes a sip   & rests
back against the pillows
I hold her hand
she quiets & relaxes
"breathe through your nose for the oxygen," I say
"in through your nose   out through your mouth
close your mouth and breathe in through your nose . . . "
She is drifting   her mouth a wide circle   in which
her small perfect tongue   like a still lake   ripples

body's deterioration parallel as direction

or   her cup flies across the kitchen

On days she rises late or early I fix her breakfast after clothes prep, back cream,
dressing, slippers, hair combed, hearing aid on.

I wheel an oxygen canister into kitchen and help readjust the nose tube and over
her ears. Her glass of orange juice to start.
She mixes bits from four boxes of cereal into her bowl. No milk, she likes it
crunchy. Blueberries, raisins, her prune a day. I cut up a peach. The strawberry
jam that she delighted on her toast yesterday, this morning is too sweet, too salty.
Her coffee w/cream, cup so difficult for her to hold steady now, has to be piping
hot. I reheat it in the microwave several times. She likes the short little Jimmy Dean
breakfast sausages, blueberry Eggos, occasionally a simple omelet. A meal both
busy and slow.   I set her daily pills out for her, ice water, and cut-up banana.

Then we wrap legs, red sandals strapped, sit outside, ice in water bottle, rolling
oxygen canister, lavender gardening hat, sunglasses, long sleeved shirt for sun,
pillows in lawn chair,   so soon   too hot,   come back in,   bring all.
Get swamp cooler going with added ice, toothpick, another pillow to her rocking
chair, a chocolate chip cookie.
"Can't breathe,   more air!"
Open front door. Open windows. Switch to house oxygen generator.
"How's that?"
"Better."

"I'm going outside for a minute," I say.
"What for?" she wants to know.
"Too hot," she cautions. "What are you going to do?"
"I need to saw a dead branch off the little Summit Ash," I explain.
"Come back soon," she says   & adds "Be careful."

I laughed so hard   my eyes wept

"Not like the last pizza we had.
There was just one thing on it.
Only 1 thing on it!"

then
"Did you say you ordered pizza with the
sauce that prevents aging?"   she questions.

that same train
ironically
later   that same day   robbed
by   different robbers

crisis night
ate at 7 — too late
open windows
close windows
too hot   too cold
get up   sit down
get up   sit down
wars with the pillows
needs ice in her water
leg rubs back rubs
needs shades raised
then lowered
bottoms of feet rubs
can't breathe
get gum   get 7Up
needs more ice
bring in standing fan   and set up
Shut off standing fan too chilly
more pillow fluffing   positioning
layers of pillows that won't behave
some nights   we die several times   a night
some nights

"There is no story that is not true," said Uchendu.

—Chinua Achebe, *Things Fall Apart*

"Who are these people?"   she asks
"What people?"
"The ones that come in here at night. They stand
in the doorway   talking."
"You must be dreaming them."
"no, No, they are real people.   They sleep in here.
Some of them sleep on the floor."
"Do you recognize any of them?"
"no, I don't know them. One is a tall man. He stays
in the doorway talking.
The women are older with grey hair.   I thought
I heard you talking to them."
"no, I haven't seen them."

"One came in with you last night."
"with me?"
"Yes,   he was behind you."

all duets
fracturing

I tuck her oxygen cord   over the coat rack above the doorway
through the title page of *The Kitchen God's Wife*   on top of the bookshelf
so she won't trip on it   getting out of bed   during the night

sweating into

what is more beautiful than a summer's darkening twilight

On this remote porch   salt plans drift
so much indentation   whose house could now resist   such
granular

I came to realize
that it was not "a break" I was experiencing
not "a vacation" not "a rest"   but instead
I was in the process of healing   of healing
from an affliction I had suffered   from
my childhood   and that by the inconceivable vagaries
of fate   I had been given this   second chance
to heal

how is the moon so round
if it does not roll

Called awake   3 a.m.
"Take this cover off me   it's too heavy!"
"This quilt is feather light tho   & it's very cold tonight."
"Get it off me,   too heavy!"
I fold it back   rearrange the sheet & lay Winnie's shorter
crocheted prayer blanket   atop her legs & feet
"I'm freezing," she pines, "Get me a lighter blanket."
"This is the lightest cover we have…"
"Why are you standing there with your hands in your pockets!
Help me!"

Actually my pjs have no pockets
It's 3 a.m.   it's 12 degrees outside
I'm so tired   thru blinds
a loopy moon   stares at me

I unfold the comforter wistfully   & gently open
it back over her

"Are you mad you had to get up?" she amends.

The Stations of Her Cross   **her way of the cross**
Via Dolorosa
            her given name   **Our Lady of Sorrows**

I   Riding her pony
            bareback to a
            one room schoolhouse

II   Divorced she wasn't
            allowed into heaven

III   Insisting she be driven to
            emergency at midnight
            stomach attacks
            feeling better even
            as we check in

IV   Reciting poems she'd
            learned in high school
            giving me intro to *poesis*
            lyric to my ear

V   Us lugging oxygen canisters
            lassos of tubing
            on train trips between
            Denver and Truckee

VI   Our road trips navigating
            dusty hot summers
            makeshift roadside stands
            peaches melons avocados
            crawling the Grapevine
            up California's belly

VII   Falling into the donut hole
hit with the true cost
of Eliquis

VIII   Going with her beloved dad
on farm tax inspector visits
(he kept the ledgers for the county)
inviting the farmers into his car
he would simply let them
disclose what they felt fair

IX   At Park Burger with Barbara
and I where she raged against
the metal chairs   the light

X   Depression drought dust storms
wrapping in a wet sheet to breathe
to sleep   freeing the horses   the
livestock   to find their own water

XI   Dressing for church
putting on lipstick at the dresser's
oval mirror farm bedroom

XII   Being able to name
every farmer in
every barn on
the way to town
who'd hanged himself
during the Great Depression

XIII   Dancing in a twirling
full flower skirt

XIV   Walking hots on California's
 racetrack fairgrounds circuit
Vallejo Stockton Bay Meadows Sacramento

bleached peaches

lasix
eloquis
metoprolol
potassium
naproxin

Washington Nationals just won the World Series
6 to 2   over the Houston Astros

Sports are her job   especially baseball and football
San Francisco   her beloved town   Giants and the 49ers
games we tarried late to view

ice water
toothpick
kleenex
oxygen
cookie

16 degrees outside

or

"…and then they understood that José Arcadio Buendía was not as crazy as the family said, but that he was the only one who had enough lucidity to sense the truth of the fact that time also stumbled and had accidents and could therefore splinter and leave an eternalized fragment in a room."

—from *One Hundred Years of Solitude*, Gabriel Garcia Márquez

Rigors of the bedroom   loom
taking off the torture compression socks
take out small hearing aids
so scary for her to stand now
to brush her teeth   & wash up
then sit on her bed undressing   blouse & silk undershirt
rub cream onto her back   pull on pj top
then off with pants & undies   stand up
sit down   stand up   sit again
pj'd   she step stools into bed to sit & put on face cream
coconut lip balm
I place ice water close
put her phone on its charger
Kleenex within reach
toothpicks
fluff pillows & bed clothes
hand her blessed-by-the-pope rosary
rosary case reachable on night stand
set face cream where it won't get bumped off
pillow under her legs
set up oxygen
blanket layered over feet   to pull up
sheet up & folded
she frets if covers pulled up feel heavy
Winnie's crocheted prayer   blankets her feet

"Don't go.   Stay   & talk awhile.
Are the lights on? How many lights are on?"

I count them for her:
painted camel skin night light
wall plug light
bright hall light
her shaded bedside lamp
bathroom rouged-paper light

"could you rub behind my ears"

above us clouds flee southward
       grounded   our wind blows north

her hair blows forward
mine blows back

mark a line   on a
milk white plank table
anchoring a stasis of modality

pillowed in fabric   swaying
upward   in gathers and drapes
arms   emerging through bouffant
unbridled   she   unlike all others

the pt & ot girls arrive   lean   celestial
tiny hoops of silver   line the curves
of their ears   bracelets of pewter &
turquoise   muscle skeletal cardiac
fulcrums   of movement   they
parachute out of normal sky
self-winding   counting repetitions

she   palimpsest

once carried me   a babe in arms
an infant   to see Man o' War
"No other horse ever won such fame . . . "

her   exaltation

"I want to go back to the way I am"
                she warbling sang

We   shaking out bedclothes
put on her good balance tennis shoes
oxygen in tow   we roll to kitchen

bowl & spoon & morning oat crunch
raisin bran   & cheerios

she shakes a bit of each in her bowl   sprinkling on a spoonful of muesli
eating it dry w/just a dab from the small pitcher of milk

blueberries   strawberries blackberries raspberries

she loves cut up peaches   and bacon   Eggo waffles
hot coffee w/half & half   toast and jam
her prune a day   and extra raisins

her arm jerks hot coffee against the wall
cools into her aproned lap

a refill coming up

Mrs. Leanie   **was Dan Campion & Ellen Phalen's daughter**

"This is the biggest mess I ever saw!   Why
do they think they can do that?"
"What?"
"come in here and sleep on the floor."
"Mom, you're dreaming."
"Maureen, I'm not!   a guy came in took his shirt off
and laid down on the floor
then 2 kids came in…
I'm not sleeping. How can I be dreaming   if
I'm not sleeping!"

"well, they're gone now.   Try and get some rest."

tu da lu Buckeroo
  a dust-up

Having gotten her all set for the night
I make up my couch bed   check her again
say goodnight   and a kiss on forehead again
fall into sleep in my bed   only to hear
about an hour later   her calling me
I lurch up   flurry into her bedroom
"Maureen   where are you? Aren't you coming in
one more time to say goodnight?"
"I did already"
"No   you didn't"
"Yes   remember I "
"No   you didn't come in"

I retuck her into the covers

"What were you doing?   Didn't you hear me calling?"
"I was sleeping   I was sound asleep"

a glass of 3 cards

           data

lip balm
Tums
talking clock
stepping stool &
rosary

grasps   a curvature confessional
its bands of slanted bars of green
through shades   of

day breaks   you & I
on a kitchen wall
two heads bobbing   a sea of white cotton
auburn   & grey   flounce pillows
   chuckling
Sandy at bed foot
snaps our photo

now
without
staging
lighting
we seem to float
your talking clock
your stepping stool to bed

there are   four pillows w/cases
a white one
2 pinkish mauve
one a dark navy w/2 thin red satin ribbons sewn near the bottom opening

or   she   "what cell am I in?

I'm in jail!"

"Please somebody help me
I can't get up
Get me out of here
Get me up   get me up
Let me out of here
Please somebody help
I can't take it"

Is it bed or body she rails against?

the edema causes her legs to weep continuously
always wet   towels & wrappings   soggy
she rips at her pjs
pulling covers & clothes off her body

What comfort am I   calming   soothing
reassuring the lights are on   the windows
open

At dawn she falls asleep

Neither dozy moths   nor   their gauzy swarms
                penumbra   bundling thru shadow

"Do you see it flying up there   near the ceiling?"
"No, what is it?"
 "the night bird   up in the corner   near the ceiling . . . "

Two earrings dangle from a fork prong
fussy occupation   but up close
volant   somewhere above her bed

one of many shades   arriving mute   of
darkened silk   Her wingéd fabric   tortuous
shortsighted   drawn to cadence

highlights vary   crisscross unstable mishmash
no surface flat enough   off-kilter shadow
bending voices   ignoring

what seethes within that plumage
sucks from the room   all oxygen
vegetation thick as thunder   knots between us
into some   exotic vacuum

while cicadas shed

**she says   she now realizes   she
doesn't like zucchini**

Packed and ready for our train trip back to mom's cabin home in Truckee's high
Sierras we saunter out   into midsummer warmth   a late afternoon stroll
around the block unleashed winds have rolled through the night before   leaving
branch parts twigs   still-leafed ripped-away stems   bits of bark   littering the
sidewalks in places   Mom proceeds slowly with her cane   I do foot sweeps
before us to clear a safe path for her   small innocuous appearing twiggy bits
crackle under our steps   She wears her new blackleather summer sandals
we prattle lambent   on our upcoming departure

Her left foot rolls on a thin stem with a pointed chipped tip which slides
thrusts into her right instep   between her sandal's wide straps   punctures a hole
Even as I catch her   blood already makes quick spurts from the tiny opening
I reach down to quell the bleeding   panicking that she takes the blood thinner
Eliquis   I don't have my cell with me   we midway around the block   the
bleeding significant
                                        She swats suddenly and cries out—a yellow flying
insect a wasp   a yellow jacket   has discovered the blood   All at once an
entire colony of them are upon us   whirling around us   mad for the jerking
red   vampiric in crazed shattering frenzy I pull her arm over my neck and half
carry her   swept frantically   toward the alley shortcut to our backyard gate   a
gang of yellow jackets hangs on   stinging   swarming but most start to fall
back   satisfied with the pooling splotches of crimson   we leave behind

Once inside the closed gate they are gone   I sit mom on a lawn chair   elevate
her leg   rush out ice   towels   band-aids   water   first aid kit   bandage gauze
Not expecting success I grab my cell but   elevating her leg and ice miraculously
stop the bleeding   A sudden calm falls   neither of us speak   Only the
wailing of our crashing hearts   audible   we wash off our stings   I apply Tea
Tree antiseptic cream   bandages on her twig puncture

                    I'd flung mom's sandal to
the deep side grass   in our emergency haste   It was soaked with blood   the soft
sole cushion bloated and dripping

I would submerge it in water   wash-squeeze   wash-squeeze   to no avail   Still
swollen it would harden to a ruddy plaster

Next morning assembling our wounded bodies   my mother's foot bandaged   in a
soft tennis shoe   we embark on our return   to her high Sierras

Sediments' looped cordage

Unable to procure even an interview   for any well paying job
the sole support of her three children   my mother
replaced her given name   with just the first initial on her resumé
right away she got a call   When she arrived for the job interview
the two fellows were taken aback   "We didn't know
you were a woman!   We can't hire a woman for this work."
It was a timekeeper job at a missile base
My mother was sharp   intelligent   competent   They hired her

I suspect it didn't hurt   she was a knockout too

caregiver's log 7.27.19   home in Denver
                mom in Truckee for a few days   without me

Mom calls
her caregiver didn't show up
no one has refilled her daily pillbox
she has no pills today

At the kitchen window   I watch
a dinosaur next door hiss & stretch out its metallic neck
scooping deep into soil above a sewage drain pipe
black cords where its mane might be glisten in the torrid afternoon sun
it sways   rears   trunk up over truck bed   dropping a maw full of dirt
from its jaws   Rumbling beeping scooping heaving   shaking grit
into the truck bed

My brother calls   enroute to ER
mom's legs swelled up suddenly in a couple of hours both legs
he and Jacki sitting right there talking to her
visiting Steve my ringer was off
declaring infection doctor has put her in the hospital
on antibiotics and back on her diuretics
I have to return   my little break   broken

Some days later
Diana & Alvin pick me up at train station main street Truckee
Arriving at the cabin I find mom out of the hospital but
her legs still severely swollen
she appears aged in the short time I was away   or maybe
I've been away long enough that I can notice how frail and pallid she is
I put things in order
& make coffee   cook dinner   set up pills   wash her jacket
make prescription calls, etc.
her neediness calls for me   if I'm away more than a minute.

I take a quick shower. Put her legs up   prepare clothes, etc. for early
church   make her bed   cream on her back   find 49ers football game on
tv   set her alarm $ in church envelope

every breath she takes floats
on an audible moan.
she's glad I'm here   she's realized   she can't do it alone

rub my back   rub my toes   rub my forehead

caregiver's log   Saturday 8.17.19

So hard to believe I arrived back in Truckee just over a week ago. A week of crisis, doctor visits, oxygen tanks, prescription pill changes, and lovely visits from neighbors and mom's dear lifelong, well, Truckee long, friends.

We went to the doctor early Wednesday. Doctor increased Lasix to twice a day, 40mg each. Went over labs, oxygen use. I got in trouble for not giving mom sufficient Lasix. I, fearing for her kidneys. The doctor, fearing for her heart.

Thursday Erin came and cleaned. Meals on Wheels for mom's lunch. I do laundry. Diana drives us to hospital for mom's lab work and stays to visit.

Friday, our right hand helper, Jacki, drives us to our appointment with the doctor to check kidney function. Kidneys holding their own, but when checking mom's oxygen level the oximeter won't register a reading. Finally it appears to work, but the number is ridiculously low. "This is not enough oxygen to sustain life!" the doctor alarms. Jacki and I look at each other and then at mom. "Yet she lives!" we proclaim in unison to the doctor. Doctor C. says mom has to go back into the hospital. "Oh No!" Jacki, mom, and I shout in unison. We argue that the oximeter often doesn't function on mom because of her atrial fibrillation. We all plead. Mom refusing to go back into the hospital. Finally we are able to warm mom's fingers enough for a reading of 88, which is not great, but the doctor is willing to let her come home if we keep her on oxygen all the time and stay on the Lasix morning and evening, 40mg. And we'll need to do labs before our next appointment on Monday! to check her vitals again.

Later at home Julie, Kapra and Ketric, best next door neighbors for forever, drop in to visit.

loading the washing machine I slowly checked them all

She would stuff her pockets with Kleenex
plaid shirt pokes   double cargo pants pouches   skinny jeans insets
hidden jacket pods   One night   belated   doing laundry
I missed   a pocket   miniscule bits   of flakey tissue
clung   covering her clothes   teeny snippets of ragged white   stuck
everywhere   I shook each apparel &   out   under the stars
tall pines   huffing   puffed in their drowsiness   while I waved a wild snow
of Kleenex   into the august dark

Toaster on a tightrope

What's wrong with me!   why don't I get better?
         Calling "Maureen   Maureen   where are you?"

Herself awkwardly
                  counting pills

I cooked dinner
We watched the Giants game   She began
having breathing problems   stomach so hot
I adjust the oxygen nose piece
position the fan
ankles swelling
the night worsens
She wakes   can't breathe
Is the window open   Is the door open?
can't breathe   panic rising
raise oxygen level
give her a Tums and ½ Lasix
prop on pillow balconies   heaped mauve&cotton
rub the lavender and sandalwood lotion on her back and ankles
as dawn blurs the darkness
set her up in the comfortable rocking chair
in the kitchen   another Tums   & second Lasix ½
call Nancy   we won't go to church this morning   no sleep
at 10   she's up &   coffee   slowly breathing

big puffy pine tops
in the solitary afternoon
a squirrel snaps a branch   that falls
knocking through other branches
my mother and I chat softly
the day has clouded over
summer's coming to a close

**I'd hire a cook
mince a scallion
boil a whale's tooth**

gusts bunt the pine tops
flat fir boughs whirl   float back
carve   a circle   sway
in place

sloppy sails   (low slung)
A tad too oversized
flirting

braces
hymns

this roof is hers

**She had worked as a Timekeeper for the Titan I   &   Titan II missiles
a woman   never allowed in the underground silo office**

Nights   are the hardest

She won't get ready for bed before 9:30 (& it takes about an hour
and a half)
I take off her oxygen nose piece
Help her stand at sink
Prepare her toothbrush with fennel toothpaste
(not spearmint not peppermint!)
adjust water faucet
she brushes her teeth for 15 minutes or more
So Long!
Readjust water temperature   & ready her washcloth w/soap
(only Dove will do!)
stand by   hold her up
towel hand off
she's exhausted & sits in hall chair to rest
I pull off her tight leg wrap stockings and shoes & put on wooly slippers

help her take off clothes & with pjs
walk her to bed
I rub lotion on her back and arms

Build her extra pillows tower
Turn her covers back
step stool & much scooting and lifting to upright position against
the pillows
the effort wears her out
Now she can't breathe needs air   "need air! Quick! Now!"
I arrange apparatus on her nose   turn on oxygen compressor
It's loud   a deep bass thud
she thinks she hears someone walking downstairs
I explain it's the compressor pumping intervals

its intermittent thud like spaced foot falls
together we position another pillow under her legs to lessen the edema
and slide a towel under to soak up their weeping
I rub lavender oil on her ankles and the bottoms of her feet   slowly & long
"How do they look? How swollen?" she asks of the edema
"Do we have to wrap them for the night?"   I always say "no,
just during the day." She is always relieved.
She would refer to the compression stockings as the torture socks
"Try to relax," I suggest. But she has a hard time doing that at night.
I put ice cubes in her water bottle in the kitchen. When I set it on her nightstand
She checks "Is it cold!"   "Yes, I put ice in it."
I hand her her face cream
her rosary & case
her chapstick   her toothpick
Plug in her cell phone to recharge
Kleenex near to reach
Fold blanket so she can reach & pull it up later in the cooling night
snap on the nightlights
"Is the window open?"
"Yes."
"I can't feel any air."
"It's wide open."
"Is the door open all the way?"
"Sure is."
"Is the fan on?"
"Yes."
"There's no air in here."
"Close your mouth and breathe through your nose to get the oxygen."
"Is the hall light on?"
"Yep."
"Is the bathroom light on?"
"Yep."
"I'll check back in when you're finished praying," I say.   I'm so tired.

"Can't you just sit awhile now?"

"uh sure, I can do that."

blasts of blazing sunset

attack her red sandals

"Who's that boy?"
"What boy?"
"There. In the kitchen. He's smoking."
"Smoking?"
"Holding a bowl."
"Is it . . . the bowl smoking?   Do you know him?"
"no."
What's he wearing?"
"a shirt and pants."
"What color are his clothes?"

"I don't know.   he's vanished now."

In space   surface tension will force
                    a small blob of liquid   to form a sphere

O went   stiff tulle
rhythms gone haywire
Cicadas twilling timber   beetles
at the grapevine   sultry   chewing
an almost violence in these clouds

a witness goes missing
   translucent as a porcelain
with binoculars on the future   in
her hand

Eyesight failing
her independence casts a spell
as she needs me read her B of A statement
questioning every entry   & forgetting
questions me again on same   I repeat
addition subtraction final balance date
a layer cake of confirmation
her balance after each check signed
She worries will there be funds enough
health ins medicare prescription pills
utilities for her cabin home in Truckee   where
only Holy water rising   Holy   Holy Holy water rising
no one is living now

occasionally   among the   snowy bedclothes
        flurries shifting   Minnesota fence lines

"I've got a problem   my rosary's gone   I can't find it."
We hunt sheets   & pillows' undersides

"Oh wait   No, no, it's ok   we put it in the case
it's right here on the night stand."

airplane crash
                   near   the doll's head

to feel the length of her body again
as I lifting   when she bent   her bending

No compass   needing   on   sidewalks
We don't have   nowhere to go

scarlet witches   did I have a father   no
nobody there   we just walk   handfuls of
ditch lilies   clouds thin as stitches   whose
mariposa tulip   neon hedgehog cactus

chiaroscuro cold case   spits warm water   hair
barbered in a boy's cut   she wore her brother's
hand-me-downs   of flesh
where once these toothpick   arms
buried a face in a horse's mane   I am her secrets now

fling two windows wide   to a vast crystal dark
to the Butterfly Nebula   3,800 light-years away
jets & gas bubbles peel off its stars   stellar winds
slam its nebula   her chaos   "I'm a mess! why
don't I get better?"

chapstick
rosary
face cream
pillow pile

ice water
toothpick
tums

bedside science stories

"Once upon a time, there was a rainforest
near the bottom of the world . . . "

"Are we going home now?

  I need to get out of here.   Let's go!"

She fired me the first night I insisted she wear
the adult diaper to bed.
"No." she finaled
I insisted
"I want someone else who works here," she said

"Were you dreaming?"

"I dreamed we all got throwed in jail."

Yesterday Hospice supplies arrived
a small foldup wheelchair
a snazzy wheeled walker w/brakes, basket & seat
new set of oxygen supplies w/quieter compressor
Melatonin for sleeping
nasal spray for nose drip
&   a raise and lower bed

last night was horrible
the bed just didn't work for her
finally put her in my bed   & retired back to the couch
no real sleep till early a.m.
then she called me every hour till dawn
"what can I do?   what do you need?"   I whimpered
"I just wanted to see you,"   she said

to many in the Midwest   it was still called supper

It's libraries   what people won't lay bare
to one another   she   phantasmagorical
only repertoire   blackened inventory   bosky
conversations   left one   tangled in bush

"Gypsy" to her girl gang   riding bareback
miles of Minnesota prairie   & high grass ditches
coming home by moon
letting the horses find the way

overhead
her galaxy   her milky way   stretching
a hundred thousand light years across

Pam:
"Last time I hung out with her
on Kentucky Derby Day   we
were mad about the crap call on the winner
she was so funny   she was pissed   she
cracked me up!"

youngest of 4   she the one of 2 sisters
who learned to drive   if a machine
part was needed   the men sent her to town
to pick it up   she attired in a brother's
hand-me-downs   straight black hair in
a boy's cut   Once she wore
a dress   the clerk stared   startled
wavering "Do you have a twin brother?"

The night she died   I
came into the room   sat
holding her face
in my hands

She was always stylin'   **or**
         wardrobe I couldn't part with   **yet**

         so bruised of

she'd insist something fit   she'd say
it didn't fit when we got home
"This doesn't fit   need a new one"
Taking her shopping became so hard
It had to be fast   it had to be 100% cotton
Made in America   snaps not zippers   or
buttons   no elastic   had to have real pockets

stacked up   great clothes we'd bought for her
in piles   shapes & colors
oil cloth rayon blue pink white patched rain jacket
Truckee winter's sheepskin fleece cloud pullover
favorite grey & salt striped jacket w/hood
fuji fancy jacket fog colored w/ bulb appliques bright yellow
floral print jacket trumpeting verdure leaves   paprika & Japanese roses
snap button cowgirl shirt I found for her in Truth or Consequence NM w/
snowy swiggles   tex-mex stitches of red threads on blue
her well worn snap button cowboy shirt a birthday present from Sean w/
inset embroideries mauve & cinnamon on sleeves and collar
Kyran's "Mars Science Lab" fleece jacket deep pink she wore so proudly
& "Mars Science Lab" vest in dusty magenta deep lilac
postmodern snappy black & white round-checkered jacket   black trisected
circles on white w/edging on color and pockets   *fashionistas* we
shopping   together in San Francisco
her blue striped short-sleeved   peppered in black embroidered   palm trees

folds of the dish towel

Time never stops   only we stop
we die   Katie emails

Ulysses says: " . . . stop referring to the ashes as your mother.
It's not her. It's just ashes. She's gone."

When you clap your hands   vibrations of air molecules travel
in a wave   causing variations in pressure   how long
do these   various frequencies   hang   in the air

round her Celtic green urn
saints and hauntings   of my Irish girlhood

miracles   rosary   sacraments   psalms
confession prayers liturgy myths   scripture   requiem

pale ghosts   of her mother's   stories

When I was in high school, my two brothers younger, my mother was a working, single parent, sole provider for our family. One rainy morning as she dashed, in recently bought galoshes, laughing, to catch the bus for work, I wrote this little poem about her.

My mother
A child of newness
In black rain boots running